YinYang

A refreshing way to percolate ideas of a different nature

Dedicated to coffee drinkers everywhere.

Contents

Brewing the new - take the time to sit and sip coffee.

A moment mingled with new flavours of consciousness.

Sipping the sublime - with the caffeine of creation.

Ideas to go - filtering thoughts stirring in the new.

A moment to gather the new as the path is resumed.

Brewing the new

Take the time to sit and sip a coffee, aromatic, rich, full flavoured.

An easy coffee moment,

mingling new flavours

with new consciousness.

1

Ideas of a different nature,

foster form of another kind.

Think like love rising.

2

Awareness in the present moment -

simply signs to movement.

3

The universe is a dance in correspondence.
Relationships, the breeze that keeps us aloft.

4

Relationship sails on the sea of unity.

Like the wave creates of itself.

5

Receive instead of plan.

Respond without first interpreting.

6

Expect willingness.

Think without the barriers of time.

7

Willingness -

cause and effect, giving and receiving,

occur as one.

Fear -

unwillingness to receive.

8

Consciousness -

the movement of being into form.

Being, is like love is

    embracing.

The voice of divinity to itself.

9

Present -

being all as you are.

Like a choir,

every cell joining in harmony.

10

Thoughts joined hear music.

Think without the need for form.

11

Coalescence - light expanding itself.

An out of pattern interval in time, intersession.

12

All things come to serve.

To use is to separate, to serve is to embrace.

13

Miracles are a natural consequence of coalescence.

Reality outside the pattern of ordinary time.

14

Identity - no longer form, flows from life itself.

Source replaying itself.

15

Be as nature ever giving, ever receiving.

Self union - the ability to resurrect in form, now.

16

Spacious, indivisible, invisible - oneself

Like a building with no frame.

17

Expect coalescence.

You are your own wings.

18

Dedicate all thoughts to unity.

Focus on continuously consistently choosing.

19

Oneself -

unadulterated by outside influence.

Source remembered arises, replacing perception.

20

Beauty still reigns. We together, are the heart beat of the world.

Sipping the sublime

with the caffeine of creation.

What we perceive (the world) is a result not a cause.

Seek not to change the world but to change one's mind.

*Submission brings nothing,
it is ego's way of limiting.
Best then to look beyond one's beliefs and limitations.*

Reality needs no cooperation from us to be itself.
Lay down the burden of denying truth.

Where there is a word there is a will,
Source reaches us directly without need for interpretation.
Act instantly upon all intuitive ideas.

*A thought is a tremendous physical force.
To think is to have an effect,
therefore be mindful of intentions.*

*Thought is the body's most powerful
instruction, we all experience the effects of
our thinking.
We are without neutral thoughts.*

In order to find our place in the infinity of being, we must be able to both separate and unite, yet remain separate from nothing and no one.

Peace is a state where love abides and seeks to share itself.
  Side with peace.

It's not what we think about, but how we think about it.
Witness your inner dialogue.

*An unrecognised belief
is a decision to war in secret.
We have no need for secrets.*

Other people's opinions are interesting, however only personal opinion matters, our opinion creates our life.

When we stop fighting & start acting the energy of intention is released. We do not want. We do not hope. We intend.

What we believe to be truth is often a defence against it.
Yet there is nothing to defend or protect.

A decision is a conclusion based on everything you believe.
Let words and actions align.

*In everyone we see, but a reflection of what we have chosen to have them be.
Perceive no differences, just for a day.*

*Surrender is the container into which grace flows.
Make the sacrifice of fear.*

All our external limitations are images of our own fears.
Unbind yourself from rules.

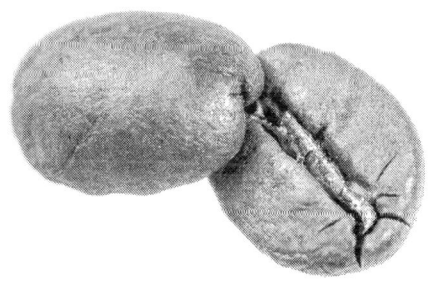

If you know how everything works, where is the mystery?
We cannot be defined nor confined.

With each belief dismantled we awaken to the free flowing energy of our genuine selves.

    *Imagine divine ordering
established in
mind, body and affairs.*

*Change is ever present.
Respect it as a force for good
In every moment, With every step,
Walk in the stream of good.*

There is no way to happiness,
happiness is the way.
Let's choose happy then,
For all ground is harvesting ground.

Without the restriction of the viewer,
(who judges and labels) the now
expands without limitation.

*All forms of crisis are resistance to change.
Yet change is our friend.*

*The past is gone and what is truly gone has no effect.
Cease the forward momentum of habitual repetitive self.*

When the self collapses and walls come down, it is not fear that remains, but freedom.
Play no part in fearful thoughts.

When we extend ourselves in giving, we give ourselves the gift.
That which we share we keep.

Nothing outside ourselves can bring happiness, there are no forms that will bring happiness.

Fear not to go within.

We do not know what hurts, or what will heal, so we must forget the world that our pasts have made.
Why not seek a future different from the past.

*Think not that happiness is ever found by
following a path away from it,
Follow thy bliss.*

We see what we believe. Be glad then, for we
can change what we believe.
Love change.

*We do not know how to look upon the world, or upon ourselves.
What we are, will tell us of itself.*

*All that we think we know is based upon past learning, We see only our thoughts projected outwards.
Let a new perception come.*

*The prerequisite for vision (inspiration) is
an empty mind.
Put aside all stories.*

*True giving is effortless effort.
So how about giving first.*

It is impossible to observe without participating.
We are the architects of our own reality,
Reality exists only where we create focus.

Keep mind awake.

Beyond right and wrong, outside of judgement, beyond rule.
This is where the heart feels.
Nurture what is new.

Every adjustment of ego is a distortion of truth and requires defences to uphold and maintain.
Do not attempt to adjust to fit the world, or adjust the world to you.

Compassion is a feeling that when cultivated, becomes a force.

Recognise it as creative power.

The world around us is nothing more and nothing less than a mirror of what we become from within. Everything we see is an effect of our thinking.

*If we want to change something we must use the conscious mind to direct the subconscious.
First, replace all fear with curiosity.*

*The universe responds to our vibrations,
our feelings,
extend radiant laughter vibrations.*

Uncontrolled thoughts are not to be feared, for we cannot stop thought. We do however have the power to direct them.

*Abundance
is not a matter of circumstances or conditions. When the mind is unified in gratitude, thoughts connect in source. Choose to be a master of the ordinary.*

Upset has nothing to do with conditions or circumstance, it is merely our reactions to them.
We are in charge of how we respond and react.

Any direction where inspiration does not lead, leads to nowhere.
Now remove all obstacles to inspiration.

*The only constant in life is change.
Change is our friend.*

*Trust resolves every problem now.
Escape from fear to peace - asking nothing
of reality, merely accepting it.*

*There is nothing to add to life, yet to receive life one must be willing not to replace it with one's own ideas.
Inspiration is the way.*

*It takes great courage to fight, but even more to surrender.
Let every doubt and fear disappear.
Observe a greater power.*

*Our past experience becomes the frame of reference by which to judge.
Cease responding in light of the past.*

*When we abstain from darkness
we emanate light.
Lets not use the past to confirm what we know.*

When we undo the thoughts that define who we think we are, we expand into the all that is.

See the all that is in everything.

Having a negative thought is not a problem as long as one extends the cure. In this instant, simply suspend judgement entirely.

*Use no relationship to hold you to the past.
Let each one
each day,
be new again.*

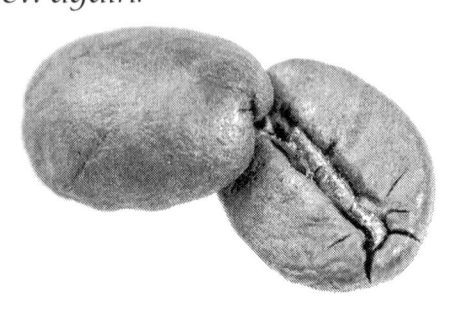

*Truth can only be apprehended by the conquest of self (ego identity).
Give thanks that the all that is, is realised under grace.*

*None can withhold truth, except from themselves.
Let all things be as they are.*

*All attack perceived is in the mind and where it begins it must end.
We will receive whatever we request.*

Miraculous events are part of an interlocking chain of forgiveness. Have a little willingness to be free.

Without thought we can create nothing. With right thought we can create the impossible.

Nothing is impossible.

Ideas to go

Filter old thoughts.

Stir in a new view.

A moment to gather in the new before the path is resumed.

*Perception is a mirror not a truth,
truth is contrary to appearances.*

*Time is an ever present here.
All things we think we see reflect ideas.*

Thoughts, not strength, rule the world.

*Love is looking with perfect gentleness upon
each other in every moment.*

To pause and reason is to stop inspired action.

Inspiration is heard most clearly in a state of grace.
Grace begins, not in the body but in the mind.

The body is merely a tool for expression, use it only for love and it will be wholly loving.

What we are is perfect, if we would only be it openly.

What if Faith is the opposite of fear.

Allow awareness to expand beyond the physical senses.

Any mistake can be corrected if truth be left to judge it.

Faith accepts every aspect of a situation without exclusion.

There is always a way around something, the question is discerning which things to go around.

Harmlessness dissolves limitation.

Do not seek for love, simply remove all barriers resisting it.

Life is a gift, that is why we call it the present.

*Giving to receive is a limitation on giving,,
for giving and receiving are one thing.*

*What is not good is not real,
what is real (bliss) is lost when awareness is
turned to not having.*

Without defence there is nothing to attack.

What is concealed cannot be loved, so it is feared.

The main concern of ego is to perceive all guilt outside the self.

Faith makes the power of belief, where and how it is invested determines it's rewards.

Ego projects - Spirit extends
fear constricts - Love extends.

Learning is invisible, yet by perceiving what it does one recognises it's being.

The ego is certain that love is dangerous. Love is simply certain.

*What we hide we keep.
Take note that asking is sharing, not taking.*

We see what we expect and expect what we invite and we invite that which we focus our thoughts upon.

By refusing to ask, be aware you are affirming the belief that to ask is to take.

What we perceive is identity's interpretation of awareness.

It is safe to operate from the centre of self.

It is impossible to see what you do not believe.

The sense of limitation is where all apparent errors come from.

Ego holds it's beliefs/secrets close, refusing to share.

Release all comparison and competition in favour of sharing.

Beware of the temptation to perceive oneself as unfairly treated.
Each of us can be a delivery system for love.

One cannot find the light by analysing the dark.

We are awareness disguised as a person.

To awaken means forgetting what you are not.

Fear and guilt are our only enemies.

Our upsets are doorways into old thoughts and old memories.

*All pain comes simply from the futile search for what we want and the insistence of where it must be found.
We do not know what anything is for.
Hindsight easily reveals purpose.*

Without anxiety the mind is wholly kind.

When we undo the stitches that define us we expand into grace.

*Fear cannot be mastered,
real mastery is through love.
It's a great life when we don't reason.*

Our greatest expectations are realised in miraculous ways.

When we function in a state of love, our inside creates our outside. When we function in fear, our outside creates our inside.

With enthusiasm bless what you have & look with wonder at their increase.

Peace and prosperity go hand in hand.

We can expect any seemingly impossible good to come from source if we do not obstruct the channels.

Give infinite intelligence right of way.

Scarcity cannot exist where there is gratitude.

Perception seems to teach us what we see, yet it is simply the witness to what we have already thought.

Love that demands, is not love.

Thought requires consciousness, however consciousness does not require thought.

Faith is what is left when what can be stripped away, is.

Where love appears, fear disappears. Fear and love cannot exist in the same moment.

When we force ourselves, our subconscious is afraid, it is resisting.

One who holds no concept of self, can see with calm and open mindedness.

A wholly open mind is undivided and looks only upon what the present holds.

Consistent application of knowledge gives consistent results.
Whatever we can imagine, the universe can deliver.

What is seen as reality is simply what the mind prefers.

Absolute well-being is the basis of our universe.

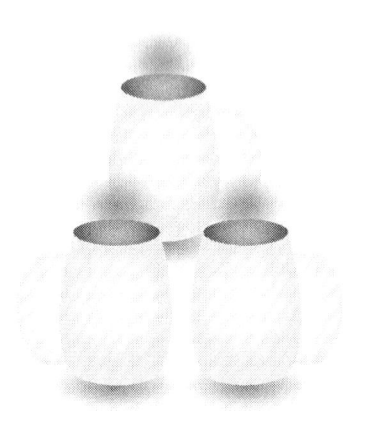

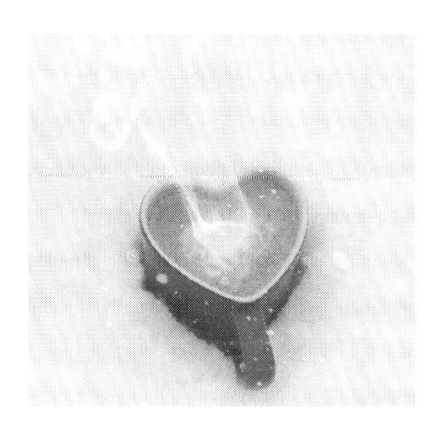

with special thanks to Hedge,

for providing gems of wonderment and an inspirational container and for the unfailing supply of liquid love beans

(you guessed it)

coffee!

And to;

Madeline & Tara for their coffee-pots.

All my glorious students, who have tried and tested, lived and grown with these words,

in gratitude to you all.

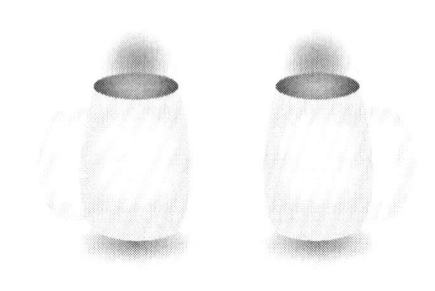

Dedicated to coffee drinkers everywhere.

The perfect coffee house companion.

We see what we believe, be glad then, for we can change what we believe.
Love change.

Wayfarer & Elfin
ideas of a different nature
www.wayfarerandelfin.com

Other titles by

Wayfarer & Film

YINYANG
BYTES

Wayfarer & Elfin

Ying Yang Bytes
data bursts on the nature of origin...

Embark upon a delightful journey with these words and images as they flow toward a natural conclusion of wholeness - sprouting ideas in consciousness, igniting mind, opening unseen spaces until clarity unfolds, fusing being and doing, gathering the jewels of life into noble-hearted living. A sense of completeness rising   the perfect launchpad for living in this multi-faceted, transient, 'instant' new world.

"My spiritual journey has been extensive, spanning many years with many teachings. This book however, is something quite different. For me, reading these messages felt like a journey – my journey – filled with wonderful healing energy sent to uplift and teach me on a level I didn't need to consciously understand – and that's gotta be a good thing!"

Sara Mendes da Costa

the trail

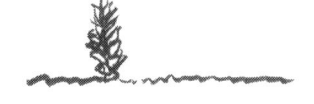

Wayfarer & Elfin

the trail

journey wordless, silent
observing the momentary forming
in transformation
simple noticing in stillness
a gentle meditation on transition
a simple wordlessness practice
gentle strolling for the greater self

"whilst looking through the trail my mind and body felt expanded yet rested.... I came to the end with heartfelt warmth, nurtured on all levels like a blanket of love, completing it beautfully, thanks for sharing ....truly touched"
PennyMay

Wayfarer & Elfin

Ideas of a different nature

www.wayfarerandelfin.com

Wayfarer & Elfin

ideas of a different nature

www.wayfarerandelfin.com

Printed in Great Britain
by Amazon